ABOUT PAY: DISCUSSING COMPENSATION

James F. Carey, CMC

A FIFTY-MINUTE™ SERIES BOOK

CRISP PUBLICATIONS, INC.
Menlo Park, California

ABOUT PAY: DISCUSSING COMPENSATION

James F. Carey, CMC

CREDITS:
Editor: **Robert Racine**
Typesetting: **ExecuStaff**
Cover Design: **Carol Harris**
Artwork: **Ralph Mapson**

All rights reserved. No part of this book may be reproduced or transmitted in any form or by any means now known or to be invented, electronic or mechanical, including photocopying, recording, or by any information storage or retrieval system without written permission from the author or publisher, except for the brief inclusion of quotations in a review.

Copyright © 1994 Crisp Publications, Inc.
Printed in the United States of America by Bawden Printing Company.

> English language Crisp books are distributed worldwide. Our major international distributors include:
>
> CANADA: Reid Publishing, Ltd., Box 69559—109 Thomas St., Oakville, Ontario Canada L6J 7R4. TEL: (416) 842-4428, FAX: (416) 842-9327
>
> AUSTRALIA: Career Builders, P.O. Box 1051, Springwood, Brisbane, Queensland, Australia 4127. TEL: 841-1061, FAX: 841-1580
>
> NEW ZEALAND: Career Builders, P.O. Box 571, Manurewa, Auckland, New Zealand. TEL: 266-5276, FAX: 266-4152
>
> JAPAN: Phoenix Associates Co., Mizuho Bldg. 2-12-2, Kami Osaki, Shinagawa-Ku, Tokyo 141, Japan. TEL: 3-443-7231, FAX: 3-443-7640
>
> Selected Crisp titles are also available in other languages. Contact International Rights Manager Suzanne Kelly at (415) 323-6100 for more information.

Library of Congress Catalog Card Number 93-73209
Carey, James F.
About Pay: Discussing Compensation
ISBN 1-56052-267-4

This book is printed on recyclable paper with soy ink.

ABOUT THIS BOOK

About Pay: Discussing Compensation is not like most books. It has a unique "self-study" format that encourages a reader to become personally involved. Designed to be "read with a pencil," the book offers an abundance of exercises, activities, assessments, and cases that invite participation.

This book is for anyone who must communicate with employees about sensitive pay issues. In clear language and using case studies, *About Pay* guides the reader toward skillful, effective methods of communicating about pay. It helps both supervisors and employees feel comfortable in the process—even when the discussion may be unpleasant.

About Pay: Discussing Compensation can be used effectively in a number of ways. Here are some possibilities:

—**Individual Study.** Because the book is self-instructional, all that is needed is a quiet place, some time, and a pencil. By completing the activities and exercises, a reader should not only receive valuable feedback, but also practical steps in mastering the techniques of effective communication about pay.

—**Workshops and Seminars.** The book is ideal for reading prior to a workshop or seminar. With the basics in hand, the quality of participation will improve. More time can be spent in concept extensions and applications during the program. The book is also effective when a trainer distributes it at the beginning of a session and leads participants through the contents.

—**Remote Location Training.** Copies can be sent to those not able to attend home office training sessions.

—**Informal Study Groups.** Thanks to the format, brevity, and low cost, this book is ideal for "brown-bag" or other information group sessions.

There are other possibilities that depend on the objectives, program, or ideas of the user. One thing is certain; even after it has been read, this book will serve as excellent reference material that can be easily reviewed.

ABOUT THE AUTHOR

A widely recognized compensation consultant, James F. Carey, CMC, has been president of Carey Associates, Inc., since 1970 and was previously a consultant with the international management consulting firm of McKinsey & Company. With over 30 years of consulting experience, he has been awarded the designation Certified Management Consultant (CMC) by the Institute of Management Consultants. His education includes a B.A. in psychology from Stanford University and an M.A. in industrial psychology from Northwestern University.

He is author of the book *Complete Guide to Sales Force Compensation* (Irwin, 1992) and numerous articles on pay planning. He conducts management seminars on compensation topics.

You are welcome to contact Mr. Carey with comments and questions about this book or for information about his consulting services at:

> Carey Associates, Inc.
> 30 Mosswood Road, Suite 201
> Burlingame, CA 94010
> (415) 347–3633

PREFACE

This is a practical guide for supervisors on how to get through the dreaded process of discussing pay with employees. Anyone who has ever worried about what to say to an employee who is not getting a merit increase will find help here. Anyone who regrets a casual remark later interpreted as a "promise" will learn how to avoid such traps. Any company concerned about a possible lawsuit, grievance, or discrimination charge based on loose talk about pay will obtain the ounce of prevention that is worth more than a pound of cure.

Hiring a new employee, giving a pay increase, or not giving a pay increase—each requires talking about pay. Senior executives and supervisors share the same anxiety when the topic of conversation is pay. This book can help any supervisor become competent, confident, and comfortable when talking about pay, one of the most important and sensitive functions of management. And the methods learned here will build the supervisor's stature in management.

James F. Carey
James F. Carey

CONTENTS

SECTION I   THE BASICS OF PAY MANAGEMENT 1
   Why Pay Is Important 3
   Understanding Employee Motivations 7
   The Objectives of Pay Management................................9
   Making Pay Changes 18
   Talking to Employees About Money 26

SECTION II   CASE STUDY EXAMPLES 33
   Studying Cases 35
   Case Study: Is That All? 36
   Case Study: Oh Promise Me 39
   Case Study: Reaching Maximum 42
   Case Study: Marginal Performance 46
   Case Study: Range Adjustment 49
   Case Study: Demands 52
   Case Study: Incentive Pay 56
   Case Study: Hiring 61
   Conclusion 67

INTRODUCTION

If you feel uncomfortable about discussing pay, you are not alone. Supervisors at all levels feel that way, even top executives. Some supervisors hesitate to talk with subordinates about pay, and some wish they could avoid the topic entirely. Employees also feel awkward when discussing their pay. However, you can learn how to communicate about pay effectively and with minimum discomfort for both you and employees.

Few supervisors have been trained in how to talk with employees about their pay. As a result, they sometimes do it poorly, saying the wrong thing and giving the wrong impression. The result can be misunderstandings, damaged employee morale, and even legal action.

This book will help any reader master the techniques of effective communication with employees about their pay. It will help the supervisor become more effective in managing and help the company get full value for its payroll dollars.

Most pay communications are simple, but every supervisor worries about facing situations that could be awkward or hard to handle. The case examples in this book are based on real-life incidents and include the problems that can arise.

To get the most from this book, take the time to write your own responses to the questions that are asked. Omit any that do not apply to you or your organization. It helps to discuss the cases with other supervisors and compare ideas and approaches.

QUIZ: TEST YOUR KNOWLEDGE

Now, as a supervisor, what are your perceptions of the importance of pay? (Answers are below.)

		True	False
1.	Payroll is one of the largest business expenses in almost all companies.	☐	☐
2.	Hiring cheap labor and weeding out poor workers can be a cost-effective way of finding exceptional workers.	☐	☐
3.	Most employees are interested only in their own pay, without regard to others.	☐	☐
4.	Your success as a supervisor depends on your employees.	☐	☐
5.	Pay is second only to production schedules in affecting costs and employee sensitivity.	☐	☐
6.	Logically seeking the maximum income for one's labor helps employees keep emotional issues out of employment decisions.	☐	☐
7.	Negotiating a pay decision can symbolize power and control for both supervisor and employee.	☐	☐
8.	Being an advocate for employees against management increases your leadership capabilities.	☐	☐
9.	As a supervisor discussing pay decisions with employees, you should never include yourself by saying "we" in reference to management.	☐	☐
10.	It is more valuable to the company to reward employees' needs for status and reward than their need for achievement.	☐	☐

Now read on to see why pay practice is both a tricky and important part of a supervisor's responsibilitiy.

Answers: 1. T 2. F 3. F 4. T 5. F 6. F 7. T 8. F 9. F 10. F

SECTION I

The Basics of Pay Management

WHY PAY IS IMPORTANT

Each person knows the importance of pay. However, to fully understand pay, we need to look at it from the viewpoints of:

> COMPANY VALUES
> SUPERVISOR VALUES
> EMPLOYEE VALUES

COMPANY VALUES

A company must be concerned about expenses if it is to survive, earn profits, and provide jobs. Payroll is one of its largest expenses of operating a business. In a manufacturing company, payroll (including benefits and payroll taxes) might be one-third of all operating expenses and the single largest operating expense, including those for raw material, parts, plant and equipment, power, advertising, packaging, or shipping. In a company that provides services, payroll might amount to *two-thirds* of operating expense!

Benefits such as a retirement plan, medical insurance, and paid vacation can add 20 to 50 percent to the base cost of wages and salaries. Payroll taxes for social security, Medicare, state disability insurance, and unemployment insurance add another 8 to 12 percent. For every $100 of base pay, the company's total payroll expense may equal $130 to $160. You can see why top management worries about the cost of pay.

An effective pay program helps the company attract and keep talented people. Employee turnover is expensive. It costs time and money to recruit new employees, to train and supervise them, and to correct, if possible, the errors they make. Dedicated, interested, and enthusiastic employees contribute great value, just as negative employee attitudes can produce costly disruption of operations, low quality, and poor customer relations. Pay can be a major waste or a major investment, depending on how well it satisfies employee motivations.

WHY PAY IS IMPORTANT (continued)

SUPERVISOR VALUES

As a supervisor, your success depends upon your employees. You cannot do all the work of the department yourself; employees must produce the needed quantity and quality of output. You train them in how to do the work, what quality standards apply, how to deal with customers, expected cooperation with other departments—all the elements for success of your department and the company. You depend on your employees, and likewise, they depend on you.

Keeping your employees interested, enthusiastic, and working with you helps you succeed as a supervisor. Pay is an important tool of leadership because it:

- Is tangible
- Has value to all concerned
- Can emphasize (or contradict) what you say about good performance
- Can satisfy or frustrate motivation
- Can influence how employees react to the job, to you, and to the company

EMPLOYEE VALUES

Employees come to work regularly and put forth their best effort for more than income alone. They also want to satisfy deeper needs for *achievement, status, recognition, self-determination,* and *security.* (See accompanying box.)

Those deeper motivations are affected by relations with other employees, content of the work, and treatment by the supervisor. Pay is involved because it symbolizes many of those deeper motivations. Both the *amount* of pay and the *method* of pay management (including communication) influence the degree of satisfaction an employee obtains on the job.

Emotionally charged motivations make pay a peculiar issue for employees. When an employee's reaction to a pay decision seems out of proportion to the money involved, the employee is responding to the satisfaction or frustration of one or more of those deeper motivations.

MONEY ISN'T EVERYTHING

> Lee hears that another company nearby pays higher rates for the same kind of job. The logical, rational thing for Lee to do would be to seek the maximum income. However, Lee responds to a complex mixture of motivations, more emotional than rational. Lee, like most established employees, did not apply for the higher paying job.

List some motivations that might have kept Lee at the old job:

_____
_____
_____
_____
_____
_____
_____

THE IMPACT OF EMOTIONS

> In contrast, Chris, upset over the smaller than expected merit increase, learned that a new engineer with less experience was hired into the department at a higher salary. Chris quickly took a job at another company—even though the drive is farther each day and the starting pay is a little lower.

List some motivations that might have prompted Chris to move to the new job:

_____
_____
_____
_____
_____
_____

WHY PAY IS IMPORTANT (continued)

Pay and Emotions

When dealing with employees on matters of pay, the supervisor—and top management—should remember the emotionally loaded motivations of employees. However, employees are not the only ones who respond emotionally to pay. Supervisors and top executives have been known to explode emotionally when questioned about a pay decision. Pay might symbolize power and control to them, and any question that seems to be a threat to their authority.

Leadership and Pay

Your title might be vice-president, director, manager, or supervisor, but if you oversee others you are a supervisor. As such, you are on the front line of pay management, making recommendations for pay increases and communicating with your employees about their pay. How well you carry out those responsibilities will determine how well the pay program helps you and your company. No other area of management responsibility influences so much cost and so much sensitivity.

Managing pay effectively can be difficult, especially if the company has a poorly designed pay program. Perhaps you wish your company had different policies, procedures, and different pay ranges. However, until you can convince your superiors that it is time for a change, you have to operate within the existing pay program. A perfect pay program is impossible because pay planning always involves compromises among several objectives. As a supervisor, your task is to get the best motivational value possible from the tools of pay management the company provides you—even if that is difficult.

You have the opportunity and the responsibility to administer pay to improve your organization's effectiveness. In doing so, you enhance your leadership role. To your employees, you are management. If you or your employees forget that, you lose a big part of your leadership capacity. A simple and effective reminder is always to say ''we'' when talking about management and the company, never ''they.''

UNDERSTANDING EMPLOYEE MOTIVATIONS

The emotional needs discussed next are important in some degree to every employee and can be satisfied in many ways—by job content, working conditions, supervisor's treatment, pay management, and communication.

Achievement: The desire to grow, accomplish, and complete goals.

To satisfy this motivation, make merit increases and incentive awards match the level of job performance. If everyone gets the same increase or no increase, the need for achievement is not satisfied. Rewarding achievement encourages the most valuable motivation among employees.

Status: The desire to be seen as someone special.

Pay represents status both within the organization and outside, and it should correspond generally with the relative importance of jobs within the company. Status based on achievement multiplies those two motivations and greatly strengthens the company.

Recognition: The desire to be noticed and respected as an individual.

Although similar to status, it does not depend on the person being placed above others. Personal recognition by the supervisor is highly valued, yet it costs nothing and is easy to deliver. Talking about pay provides an excellent opportunity to recognize the employee—even when job performance is not exceptional. Listening helps to provide recognition.

Self-determination: The desire to feel in control of one's own destiny.

A highly regulated job provides little sense of self-determination, but the more choices the employee has in planning and conducting the work, the greater will be the satisfaction of this motivation. Discuss with the employee what it takes to get a larger pay increase or promotion, and what the person likes about the job. Also find ways to give the employee choices or flexibility in how to perform the job.

Security: The desire to know what is ahead and confidence about coping with the future.

To build security and reduce anxiety or resistance, explain in advance about a future change. Security is provided by certainty of employment and by structure and control in the workplace. High-performance companies encourage achievement and self-determination (improvement) more than security (status quo).

Exercise: Are Motivational Needs Being Met?

How well are the motivational needs of your department's employees being satisfied?

Motivation	Poor	OK	Good	Not Sure
Income	____	____	____	____
Achievement	____	____	____	____
Status	____	____	____	____
Recognition	____	____	____	____
Self-determination	____	____	____	____
Security	____	____	____	____
Other _____	____	____	____	____

THE OBJECTIVES OF PAY MANAGEMENT

Employee satisfaction is more important than any other objective in pay management. Pay must satisfy employees or the company has bought nothing of value for its payroll dollars. A poorly designed or poorly managed pay program makes it difficult for the company to hire and keep good workers and to get high quality and high output. An employee turnover rate of more than 1 percent per month may signal a poorly managed pay program. Although other factors can influence employee turnover, pay can be a major factor because of its profound effect on employee attitudes.

Exercise

What does a high turnover rate say about a company's ability to satisfy employees?

_____
_____
_____
_____
_____

What other legitmate reasons—other than a poorly managed pay program—can account for high employee turnover?

1. _____

2. _____

3. _____

THE OBJECTIVES OF PAY MANAGEMENT (continued)

Satisfaction about base pay does not mean that workers are dancing in the aisles with happiness. Pay satisfaction produces a neutral feeling—"The pay is OK." Other potentially motivating factors in the job have little positive effect if the employee feels pay is less than satisfactory. Employee dissatisfaction may show in negative remarks, complaints, and grievances. Other clues to employee dissatisfaction include:

- absenteeism
- job injuries
- indifferent approach
- union militancy
- complaints to government agencies
- lawsuits
- high turnover

Exit interviews with terminating employees and attitude surveys with current employees can help to analyze the level of satisfaction with pay.

Exercise

How does your position as a supervisor allow you to spot employee indifference toward each of the following?

The work _____

The company _____

You the supervisor _____

The customer _____

Pay Satisfaction Basics

Pay satisfaction rests on three supports. It is:

> FAIR
> COMPETITIVE
> REWARDING

The three may not balance perfectly, but if any one of them is much too short employee satisfaction will fall off.

Fair Pay

Fair pay means that pay rates *within* the organization reflect differences in job duties and responsibilities. Employees recognize that some jobs are worth more than others because of differences in skills, complexity, responsibility, and decision making required. To build fairness into the pay program, the company measures the relative value of each job by using a job evaluation committee or specialist to analyze job duties and responsibilities.

Employees know—or have opinions about—the relative value of jobs in the organization and the pay rates. When pay differences match the differences in perceived value of jobs, employees tend to feel that the pay is OK. When employees reach this level of satisfaction with internal equity, they show less interest in the pay offered by other companies.

When employees feel frustrated by what they consider to be unfair pay differences, they may:

- display negative work attitudes
- have poor attendance
- file more worker's compensation claims
- begin union militancy
- display interest in changing jobs

No company can afford to ignore internal pay fairness.

You have a good idea of the relative importance and value of jobs in your department. If the company's classification system does not closely match your idea of what is fair, let the compensation manager or the human resources director know of your concern for fairness *within* the company. *Regardless of what other companies pay for a similar job, internal fairness comes first.*

Fair Pay Match Game

Match the employee comment with the fairness issue. Issues may be used more than once.

COMMENT	ISSUE
____ 1. What counts in this company is not what you do but who you work for. ____ 2. Experience gained in this company seems to be worth less than experience gained outside. ____ 3. Complainers get rewarded here, not the quiet person who does a good job. ____ 4. We don't know how management makes pay decisions, but we have plenty of suspicions. ____ 5. College graduates get higher pay than those of us who came up the hard way. ____ 6. I would like to know why some other jobs pay more than mine. I work hard, I should get more. ____ 7. I hate to ask for a raise, but I guess I will have to. It's the only way to get one. ____ 8. The attractive receptionist earns more than the middle-aged senior accounting clerk.	**A.** *Secrecy.* Pay relationships seem to be established in an arbitrary way, without a clear procedure or explanation. **B.** *Favoritism.* Pay seems to reflect the boss's personal interest in a job function or liking for a person. **C.** *Squeaky wheel.* Management reacts to pay complaints or demands, and does not take the initiative. **D.** *Outsiders preferred.* New people being hired seem to be worth more than loyal, experienced employees who are on the job.

Answers: 1. B 2. D 3. C 4. A 5. D 6. A 7. C 8. B

The supervisor is largely responsible for:

▶ Knowing how the company's job evaluation system works

▶ Recommending merit pay increases

▶ Informing employees about their increases so they can appreciate this recognition of their performance.

When you know how the program operates, you will be able to answer employee questions (Information) and you will be more convincing about the effort made to ensure fairness throughout the company's pay program (Impact).

Exercise

Besides helping the employee, how will having information and impact benefit you the supervisor?

_____
_____
_____
_____
_____

THE OBJECTIVES OF PAY MANAGEMENT (continued)

Competitive Pay

Competitive pay, the second support for a satisfying pay program, means that your company's pay rates are *close to* the general pattern of pay in the *relevant labor market*. It does *not* mean that your company must match a salary survey average rate for every job. If the company pay rates are generally within 10 percent (above or below) a salary survey average, that is reasonably close to competitive pay.

Remember, half of all companies pay *below* average.

With generally competitive pay rates, your company can recruit new employees without too much difficulty and can retain most of them—provided that working conditions are reasonable. However, rates more than 10 percent below competitive pay may limit the number and quality of employees the company can recruit. You may still hire good workers, but it will be harder to find them and keep them. High pay does not guarantee good workers, but it gives you greater selection and a better chance of getting and keeping the people you want.

The relevant labor market might include companies outside your community or your industry. While you may not usually be responsible for defining the competitive labor market and selecting appropriate pay surveys, you have a duty to let company pay planners know of any valuable information on competitive pay you might learn. Maybe you see a pay survey in a trade magazine or you learn of pay rates or pay practices in competitor companies—pass it along.

Before you talk with employees about their pay, you need to know generally how your company plans pay rates and what it does to keep pay competitive. If the company does not have a formal program of pay orientation for supervisors, ask the responsible person how it is handled.

Labor Markets Match Game

Match the labor market where your company competes for employees in each category.

EMPLOYEE CATEGORY	LABOR MARKET
____ 1. Unskilled shop workers (e.g., laborers)	A. All companies in your city or immediate area
____ 2. Semiskilled shop workers (e.g., machine operators)	B. All companies in your state
____ 3. Skilled shop workers (e.g., tool and die makers)	C. All companies in your region (a few states)
____ 4. Clerical or office workers (e.g., accounting clerks)	D. All companies nationwide
____ 5. Technicians or drafters	E. Same industry in your city or immediate area
____ 6. Professionals (e.g., accountants, engineers)	F. Same industry in your state
____ 7. Mid-level managers	G. Same industry in your region (a few states)
____ 8. Top executives	H. Same industry nationwide

THE OBJECTIVES OF PAY MANAGEMENT (continued)

Rewarding Pay

The third support for building employee satisfaction into pay management is to reward individual growth and contribution to the job. Merit pay increases based on the employee's job performance are the foundation for rewarding pay. If all employees get the same general increase or if pay increases are based only on length of service, the company does not reward outstanding individual performance (and is not likely to see much of it). Some companies measure and reward team results but not individual performance. If the team is small and functions as a single work unit, then team-based merit increases may be just as effective in building employee satisfaction.

Your responsibility as a supervisor in a merit pay organization includes establishing job performance standards and appraising results. It works better if you involve the employees in this process. Employees generally accept and respond more favorably to goals they have helped to set.

Most companies conduct formal performance appraisals at employment anniversary or year-end reviews, though sometimes monthly or quarterly. While frequent appraisals keep employees alert to their goals and results, appraisals do take time. There is also some question about the practical value of connecting every performance appraisal directly to a merit pay increase. So, some companies conduct quarterly performance appraisals, but only the year-end appraisal guides merit pay increases.

Regardless of the appraisal schedule, as a supervisor you constantly appraise how your employees perform in:

- attendance
- quality of work
- quantity of work
- cooperation
- initiative
- customer relations

Don't keep these observations secret—regularly let employees know how they are doing and what could be done better. They want to know!

Collecting Appraisal Information

> One successful department manager was noted for the quality of detailed information in his formal performance appraisals. When asked how he did it, he pulled open his desk drawer and took out a file folder filled with scraps of paper. "Whenever something happens that I notice—good or bad—I make a note of it. At appraisal time, I dump all those notes on my desk and sort them by employee and date. It reminds me of problems created and solved many months ago, so that during appraisals I am not so much influenced by recent events or my personal liking for a person. And it gives me material to write on the appraisal form and to talk to the employee about. Usually, I talk to the employee at the time of the incident, so these notes don't come as a surprise when we conduct the formal performance appraisal. Don't all supervisors do this?"
>
> No, but they should.

How do you keep information on your employees for appraisal reviews?

_____
_____
_____

Your company may provide a budget and guidelines for merit increases, to help you to avoid the inflation of performance ratings. Without such devices, some supervisors become overly generous, for example, by setting standards or by rating everyone as outstanding to buy their goodwill. On the other hand, a supervisor may be so hard to please that no employee could ever get a high rating—a real morale breaker!

Exercise

You are the essential link between what the company wants from its pay system and what it gets. How can you establish performance standards and appraise results to get more out of each pay dollar?

_____
_____
_____

MAKING PAY CHANGES

All the machinery of pay management—grades, ranges, policies, and procedures—may be designed by others, but the supervisor is on the front line of pay management, the link between the formal pay program and actual pay practice. The supervisor plans pay changes for the department and tells employees about their pay changes. The success of any pay program depends on how well the supervisor carries out those day-to-day responsibilities of pay manangement.

Although some types of pay change might not apply in your company or your department, understanding each of them will help you deal with any question that might arise. Consider the major issues for each of these pay changes:

- Hiring
- Range adjustment
- General or cost-of-living allowance (COLA)
- Step
- Merit increase

Hiring

As a supervisor, you may be directly involved in the hiring process. In conducting interviews, you will listen to an applicant's qualifications and may be asked to detail the duties of the job. You may have to decide what pay rate to offer—a big responsibility.

The following guidelines will help you deal effectively with a job applicant when you have to decide or recommend a starting pay rate.

Remember:

▶ *The three aims of pay management are fair, competitive, and rewarding pay.*

▶ *You are not just hiring a new employee, you are making a pay decision within the total pay system.*

Your decision can affect the attitudes of other employees also.

The company's schedule of grades and ranges will guide you toward a pay rate that is in line with the pay of other jobs in the company. For the system to remain coordinated and controlled, each supervisor must follow the company's pay guidelines and policies. Incorrectly classifying an employee distorts the system and results in internal inequities that other employees will resent.

Early warning signs that your company has not kept up with competitive pay levels may show up when you recruit a new employee—let the human resources director or the compensation manager know about it.

When and how do you set the starting pay rate when hiring? If there is a single starting rate, you can mention it early in the interview. However, if you must decide on a starting rate to offer the applicant, wait until you evaluate his or her qualifications and decide this is the person you want to hire.

Don't try to hire cheap. An employee comes to work with attitudes that affect the value and length of service of the employee. Make that a positive attitude by the way you treat the new employee personally and in the pay.

Don't ask applicants what pay they want. It puts applicants in an uncomfortable position—afraid to be priced out of the job or afraid you will take advantage of a too-low asking rate. Start the employment relationship on a fair and friendly basis, but keep the initiative with you, the supervisor.

If possible, discuss pay only *after* you have determined that this is the applicant you want to hire. When you do tell *the* starting rate, don't hesitate or invite negotiation. Most people don't want to negotiate anyway. They want *you* to set the pay fairly and will respect a fair decision.

Exercise

What problems have you encountered with these factors?

- Incorrect classification: _____

- Finding noncompetitive pay levels in your system: _____

- Disclosing base pay rate before you are committed to an applicant: _____

- The other costs of hiring cheap: _____

- Negotiating pay with applicants: _____

MAKING PAY CHANGES (continued)

Range Adjustment

An increase in the pay range for a job grade is a range adjustment, which means that employees whose existing pay rate had not advanced beyond the new minimum will get an automatic pay raise that is *not* based on performance.

When you disclose the pay increase, you might also talk about each employee's job performance, but it is your responsibility to make it clear (verbally and in the paperwork connected with the pay change) that the range adjustment is *not* a merit increase. You can prevent serious, expensive trouble in the form of a wrongful discharge claim or a discrimination charge from an employee who says, "My job performance was satisfactory as shown by the pay increase I received."

Don't be tempted as a supervisor to get some extra mileage from the pay change by implying that it is based on the employee's good performance. It is deceitful to the employee, who is likely to learn the truth later. *When talking about a range adjustment, tell it straight and avoid problems later.*

General or Cost of Living Allowance

If a general pay increase is based on the Consumer Price Index, it is called a cost-of-living allowance (COLA). If your company wants you to explain a general, across-the-board increase, here are some suggestions:

▶ Call the employees together and explain the pay change to all at the same time.

▶ Explain that this is not an individual merit increase and does not reflect a positive or negative appraisal of any employee's peformance.

▶ Check for understanding of the message and answer questions the employees may ask.

Step

A step increase is an automatic or almost-automatic pay change based on time in the job. Step rate pay systems are rare in companies, but many public agencies and hospitals use this method of pay management. The employee is hired at the minimum rate for the job, called step 1. After a year, the employee's pay is increased to step 2 and so on to the top step of the pay range for the job. Successive steps are commonly 5 percent increases.

As the supervisor, you can tell the employee when the new pay rate goes into effect and congratulate the employee on his or her continued good work (if that is true) or continued service with the organization. The step increase is significant to the employee, so don't ignore it. For apprentices or trainees, a step increase might also require passing some test, in which case you can talk about the employee's progress and what is required for the next step.

With a step rate pay system, the organization may also make range adjustments from time to time to keep pay rates generally competitive. When the ranges increase, each step in the range is raised by the same percentage. If you are a supervisor in a step rate organization, be sure you understand the system and its procedures before talking with employees about their pay changes.

Quiz

Non-merit-based pay increases like range adjustments, cost-of-living allowances, and step increases reward these employee motivations (True or False):

	True	False
1. Achievement	☐	☐
2. Status	☐	☐
3. Recognition	☐	☐
4. Self-determination	☐	☐
5. Security	☐	☐

Answers: 1. F 2. F 3. T 4. F 5. T

MAKING PAY CHANGES (continued)

Merit

A merit pay system encourages good performance by rewarding it. An employee who just barely meets the performance standards for the job gets a small increase or no increase while an employee who performs well on the job gets a large increase. Most employees feel that merit pay is appropriate *if* the standards for appraising performance are fair and are understood by the employees.

A merit pay system can help the company in two ways.

▶ It obviously encourages employees to come to work on time, do their assigned tasks well, cooperate with others, and provide extra quality or quantity of output.

▶ Even more valuable is the sense of fairness it brings to the management of pay. Employees with strong built-in motivation and good work habits are attracted to a company that offers a well-managed merit pay system.

You, the supervisor, must provide four key functions in making merit increases effective.

1. Set Clear Job Performance Standards

Employees should know what is expected of them and what it takes to get a high performance appraisal. Otherwise, employees must learn the standards by trial and error, a style of supervision that has been called *retroactive expectations* because the employees hear from you only when they fall short in performance or overreach in authority. And what they usually hear has a negative tone. One of the most frequent comments from employees in attitude surveys is "I wish I knew what the supervisor expects of me."

2. Conduct a Fair Appraisal of Employee Results

Do this in relation to job standards. Informal performance appraisal happens continually, but formal appraisal is essential to a well-managed merit pay system and should be:

- Fair

- Objective

- Based on job-related results and behavior (not on the employee's traits or attitude)

- Applied uniformly to all employees, and recorded in a written record.* The written record of performance appraisals is particularly important in conection with merit increases because it establishes proof of the link between performance and pay. That proof can avoid disputes and charges of favoritism or discrimination.

3. Plan and Budget Merit Increases

This should be done within the department or work group using the company's general guidelines (see the two examples on page 24). Within those guidelines, you must work out a schedule of pay increases that will reflect the differences among employees in their performance and value to the company. The Merit Increase Guideline (see Example 1) provides flexibility for the supervisor in planning pay increases, while the budget goal keeps the cost under control. Under the simple guideline, high-performing employees can move ahead faster.

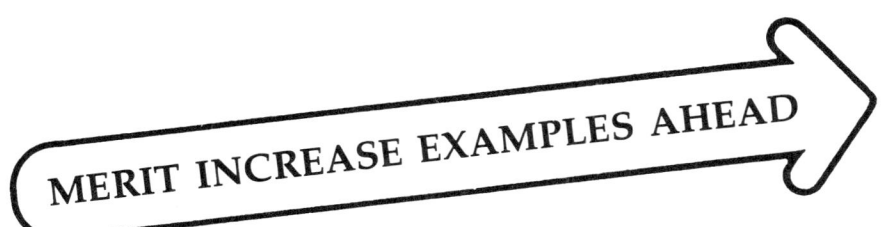

---

*For more information, see *Performance Appraisal*, by Robert B. Maddux, in *Effective Performance Appraisals*, Crisp Publications, Menlo Park, CA. 1993.

MAKING PAY CHANGES (continued)

Example 1

> ### XYZ Corporation
> *Merit Increase Guideline for 19XX*
>
> | Performance | Increase |
> |---|---|
> | Outstanding | 8.0% to 10.0% |
> | Above Expected | 6.0% to 7.5% |
> | As Expected | 4.0% to 5.5% |
> | Below Expected | 0.0% *or* 3.5% |
> | Unsatisfactory | 0.0% |
>
> Company merit increase budget this year is 5.5%.
>
> If total merit increases for department would exceed 6% or fall short of 5%, please submit a written explanation to the president.

Some companies use a Merit Increase Matrix (see Example 2), which limits the supervisor's decision making about individual merit increases and is designed to slow the rate of pay growth as the employee's pay rate rises in the pay range.

Example 2

> ### ABC Co., Inc.
> *Merit Increase Matrix for 19XX*
>
> | | Place in Pay Range | | | |
> |---|---|---|---|---|
> | **Performance** | 1st 25% | 2nd 25% | 3rd 25% | 4th 25% |
> | Outstanding | 8.5% | 8.0% | 7.5% | 7.0% |
> | Above Expected | 7.0% | 6.5% | 6.0% | 5.5% |
> | As Expected | 5.5% | 5.0% | 4.5% | 4.0% |
> | Below Expected | 4.0% | 3.5% | 0.0% | 0.0% |
> | Unsatisfactory | 0.0% | 0.0% | 0.0% | 0.0% |
>
> Company merit increase budget this year is 5.5%.
>
> If total merit increases for department would exceed 6% or fall short of 5%, please submit a written explanation to the president.

4. Communicate with Each Employee About His or Her Pay

Talking with employees about their pay provides the essential link between what the company wants from its pay system and what it actually gets. That responsibility rests with you, the supervisor.

Match Game

Match the supervisors' four key functions concerning merit pay with important results:

FUNCTIONS	RESULTS
___ 1. Set clear performance standards	**A.** Establishes proof of the link between performance and pay
___ 2. Conduct fair and documented appraisals	**B.** Helps employees know what is expected from them
___ 3. Plan and budget a merit pay program	**C.** Links what the company wants and what it gets from a pay program
___ 4. Communicate the what and the why about pay with employees	**D.** Reflects differences between the value of each employee to the company

Answers: 1. B 2. A 3. D 4. C

TALKING TO EMPLOYEES ABOUT MONEY

When you sit down to talk abut pay, the process can be difficult for both you and the employee. You, the supervisor, want to handle the situation smoothly, without mistakes, and with a cooperative response from the employee. Naturally, you are nervous about this conversation, but so is the employee. Not often does the supervisor call the employee aside for a chat, and the employee worries that it could mean bad news. Because the topic is pay, the employee's emotions rise—for the reasons discussed earlier.

Two nervous people, supervisor and employee, sit down to talk about an emotionally charged topic. How that discussion turns out will depend largely on how you handle it.

Exercise

What approaches have you used for other emotionally charged topics?

___

___

___

___

___

___

___

___

Here are some general points to keep in mind when talking with an employee about pay.

Purpose of the Meeting: The Three E's

Your conversation has three purposes.

1. EXPLANATION

- Give information to the employee.
- Help the employee understand it.
- Check that the employee does understand it. You do this every day when you give work instructions or explain a new policy. That's the easy part.

2. EXPLORATION

- You welcome response from the employee.
- The employee confirms his or her understanding, explains or persuades, and tests how you and the company will react to his or her viewpoint.

Exploration like this can be more complicated than simple information giving.

3. ENCOURAGEMENT

When a talk about pay is connected with performance appraisal, include guidance on:

- Quality of work.
- Quantity of work.
- Attendance.
- Requirements for promotion.

Assure the employee that he or she can do it. If there is no basis for encouragement about promotion, then omit that from your conversation about pay. You do not want to give false hopes to an employee if the person's ability or the organization's opportunity is very limited. New employees usually need more encouragement than do experienced workers, but everyone appreciates some. That's why the coach pats the player on the back—even a top professional.

TALKING TO EMPLOYEES ABOUT MONEY (continued)

Those three purposes—explanation, exploration, and encouragement—provide the track for your talk about pay. If you sense that the conversation is getting off the track and into other areas, like psychological counseling or legal argument, call a time out and tell the employee, "We are here only to talk about your pay. I'm not qualified to get into this other area with you. Perhaps you should talk with someone in the human resource department."

Exercise

As a supervisor, what other experience or skills in explanation, exploration, and encouragement do you bring to pay discussions?

_____
_____
_____
_____

Preparation for the Meeting

Talking about pay requires that you know what you are talking about:

▶ If necessary, review the company policy about pay before you call the employee to your office.

▶ Get the employee's pay record so you can refer to it if a question arises about the person's last increase, date of entry to the job, or other details. Proper preparation will help you talk about pay with confidence and comfort and earn you the employee's respect.

The talk about pay should be in private. If you share an office, find another place to talk, or ask others to leave the office while you are talking about pay. Close the door and shut off the telephone. No interruptions, please!

Exceptions to the Privacy Rule

There may be an exception or two to the privacy rule. If the employee does not speak your language, you may allow an interpreter to be present during the talk about pay. The best arrangement is to mutually agree on the interpreter. Select one who can translate abstractions such as "fairness," "pay relationships," and "opportunity." Tell the interpreter that this is a confidential conversation. Provide the employee with written details about a pay change and date of next review.

Another exception to the rule of privacy concerns union workers, in which case, the employee may have a right and a preference to have a union representative present when you talk about pay.

PRACTICE THE ART OF GOOD LISTENING

Talking about pay should be a conversation, not a lecture. Listen to your own part of the conversation. Are you talking *to* or talking *with* the employee? You should be talking 50 to 65 percent of the time and listening the rest.

Your Idea

Define what being a good listener means to you.

_____
_____
_____
_____
_____
_____

Listening means more than just keeping quiet, but that is a start. You don't have to carry the full burden of the conversation or respond to every question or comment by the employee. If there is a period of silence, don't feel uncomfortable about it. Let it serve as an invitation for the employee to say what is on his or her mind; then you have a real conversation going.

Interrupt only if necessary to get the conversation back on the track. Cutting in is cutting off. *Even if the employee is wrong or hostile, let the person get it out.* Think carefully about what is said and what is meant—then reply. This acceptant, open style of conversation shows that you are listening and trying to understand. It does not mean that you agree with everything the employee says. You are simply letting the person say it and you will know much more than if you had interrupted and cut off the flow of remarks and feelings.

Your questions and brief comments help the conversation flow and show that you are listening. "What do you mean?" and "I see" can keep a conversation rolling. Avoid asking questions that can be answered with a "Yes" or "No." Instead ask open-ended questions that invite the person to talk about the subject: "Tell me how you understand this," not "Do you understand?"

QUESTIONS, QUESTIONS, QUESTIONS

You can respond to the employee's questions better by learning to recognize three basic types of questions.

1. The *information question* asks for facts.
- "When will I get my next pay review?"
- "What is the maximum pay rate for my grade?"

You give the answer, or say you will get it within a few days, or tell the employee where to get the information. Dealing with information questions is easy.

2. A *topic question* is the type of question the employee asks so he or she can talk about a particular topic.
- "Why don't we get a cost of living increase?"
- "Why don't I get paid for overtime work?"

The employee may not be as interested in your reply as in his or her own comments, so don't be quick to give an answer—especially if you have already explained the matter. If you feel you should give an answer, make it short and end with "What do *you* think?" or "How do *you* feel about that?" If you're not sure whether it is an information question or a topic question, try the tactic of not answering right away. If an information question, the employee will often ask it again. If a topic question, the employee will go ahead and discuss it anyway, and the good listener gives the other person a chance to talk.

3. The *statement question* makes a statement—usually about how the person feels.
- "Do you think it's fair for the company to hire new engineers at the same pay rate I'm getting after three years?"
- "Why is it so hard to get a decent pay raise in this company?"

Beware! The emotionally toned statement question is a land mine waiting for you to step forward. The employee may not want an answer, so don't give one. But do acknowledge the feelings ("You feel upset about the smaller raise you got this year"). Then let the person sound off. The statement question is also a request for you to listen and understand, not to be defensive or agree ("I can see how you feel").

THE CLOSE

When the conversation ends, the employee should understand what action the company is taking (or not taking), the effective date, and what is ahead. You can ask the employee to summarize those points. "Tell me how you understand this—and what is next." Or you can summarize the points yourself.

Where possible, give the employee a copy of the payroll change notice or some other written record of the new pay rate and the effective date. Mention when the next regular pay review is planned.

A friendly word of encouragement and a handshake may conclude the conversation. Be yourself, use your normal style of conversation.

SECTION II

Case Study Examples

STUDYING CASES

This part contains case examples of difficult or awkward pay management situations you, the supervisor, might face.

Read each case and analyze what has happened and what is likely to happen in the future. Consider each of these viewpoints: employee, company, and supervisor. Then consider how you would handle a similar situation. Answer the quiz questions. Finally, read the commentary that follows each case.

You might not agree with the commentary in every case. However, you will have considered alternatives, and that is the way to sharpen supervisory skills. Then, when one of these difficult issues is staring you in the face, you will feel confident knowing you can handle it.

CASE STUDIES AHEAD

Case Study: IS THAT ALL?

A common problem faced by supervisors is the employee who expects a larger increase than is being granted.

Pat, the supervisor, is talking with Ali, the employee, about a merit raise:

PAT: Ali, your new salary goes to an annual rate of $30,500, starting next month.

ALI: But, that's less than the raise I got last year. And, you said my work was OK. Why is this raise smaller?

PAT: That's a normal increase for this year, Ali. Some people are getting nothing. Times have changed. Your new salary is at the midpoint of your salary range. That's about right for the position.

ALI: Well, I know salaries are not going up like they used to. But, I had hoped for more.

PAT: I tried to get more for you, but management put out a tight budget. They won't give us any flexibility. Maybe next year you can get more.

Quiz

1. How well are the employee's motivational needs being satisfied in this situation?

   _____
   _____

2. How does the employee feel about the situation and the supervisor's comments?

   _____
   _____

3. How well are company concerns being satisfied in each of these categories?

	Poor	OK	Good	Not Sure
Cost Control	_____	_____	_____	_____
Employee Satisfaction	_____	_____	_____	_____

4. Is there any issue here that could lead to a problem for the company?

_____
_____
_____

5. How well is the supervisor performing in these matters?

	Poor	OK	Good	Not Sure
Fairness of Pay	_____	_____	_____	_____
Competitive Pay	_____	_____	_____	_____
Rewarding Pay	_____	_____	_____	_____
Clear Explanation	_____	_____	_____	_____
Listening	_____	_____	_____	_____

6. What would you say or do differently?

_____
_____
_____
_____

Case Study: IS THAT ALL? (continued)

Review Commentary

The information Pat gave about the salary increase was clear and precise. The additional general information about the salary program was good but could have been more complete. In talking about Ali's position in the salary range, Pat makes no comment about the person or the job performance. Pat could have said more, but it might not have changed Ali's disappointment.

Generally, Pat was dealing with an awkward situation reasonably well—until the end. Then Pat gave up responsibility or participation as a member of management. Remember, *you* are management. It's not "us" and "them." When you talk about management and the company as "we," you enhance your stature as a supervisor.

By saying, "I tried to get more for you," Pat lowered the stature of the supervisor's job and also took something away from the employee. Ali is now sure the increase is not what it should have been and feels cheated. And Pat did nothing to help. That's not leadership.

Pat could have listened more. Silence and nods or "I understand" go a long way to easing the tension in such a situation. Listening is not agreeing, defending, or compromising. It is understanding. Every comment by the employee does not require a response from the manager.

"Maybe next year you can get more" is not a clear promise, but it is dangerously close to a promise. If Ali did not hear all the words or does not remember them accurately, he could be headed for a bigger disappointment next year. In concluding the session, Pat could have switched attention from the past to the future without a near-promise by mentioning that there is still plenty of growth opportunity for Ali in his current job. And, if appropriate, Pat could have reviewed what Ali might do to qualify for promotion to a job in a higher classification.

Case Study: OH PROMISE ME

Because you can sympathize with wanting to know the future, you might be tempted to offer an employee assurances in a way that could be interpreted as promises. This could be bad for you and for the company.

Gerry, the controller, is talking with Jamie, who was hired six months ago as a cost accountant. The performance appraisal has been completed and they are now ready to discuss pay:

GERRY: Jamie, I am very pleased with the way you are handling your responsibilities. Your new salary will start next month—a 10 percent increase. Keep up the good work. You have a great future with our company.

JAMIE: Thank you. I like working here, and I enjoy the independent responsibility I have.

GERRY: Good. When you are ready, we will set up a meeting with production to show them how we can quickly generate costs for any new packages.

JAMIE: I've been wondering. When this costing project is completed, will there be anything else for me besides data collection and routine reports?

GERRY: No need for you to worry! With your talent, you will always have a good job here. In fact, if the costing model proves to be the success we expect, you can count on moving up to unit supervisor.

Case Study: OH PROMISE ME (continued)

Quiz

1. Does Gerry think a promise has actually been made to Jamie?
   ____ Yes ____ No

2. What does Jamie expect—and when?

3. What would a court say about the company's obligation to Jamie?

4. How else could Gerry have responded?

Review Commentary

Jamie was looking ahead and felt insecure about the prospects of being stuck with routine work after completing the interesting and satisfying development project. Gerry got carried away with enthusiasm for the project and Jamie's performance on it. The way some courts view such cases, when the supervisor said, "You will always have a good job here," the comany promised lifetime employment to Jamie. Although a lawsuit is not likely now, a wrongful discharge suit might be filed years later if a change within the company or a change in Jamie's value to the company resulted in employment termination.

A former employee might or might not win such a lawsuit, but the company would surely lose the legal expense needed to defend the case. And the supervisor would lose the respect of others in the company for using poor judgment.

Gerry's promise of a promotion also may be hard to keep. The job of unit supervisor may be eliminated or another employee might be better qualified when an opening does occur. Rarely is there any good reason to designate a "crown prince" who is promised the next promotion. Such a practice discourages other employees and may hamper the ability of the chosen person to function effectively until promoted.

Most people don't expect promises. Even the person who asks for a promise probably will be satisfied with simple recognition. A statement that begins with "I believe . . ." will keep you away from stating something as fact or promise. If you *must* make a promise, put it in writing and get it approved by at least one higher level of management after review by an employment law specialist.

Case Study: REACHING MAXIMUM

Perhaps the most dreaded pay issue is talking to the employee who gets to the top of the pay range for the job. Perhaps the employee has been with the company for several years and is a good performer—even outstanding. It is difficult to tell such a person that he or she has topped out, but the situation rarely turns out badly if it is explained to the employee frankly and completely.

Supervisor Dale is talking with an employee, Terry, who is reaching the maximum pay rate.

DALE: Terry, your work has been first class and your new salary reflects that good work. Next month we are bringing you to the top of the salary range for your job, $2,750 per month, up from $2,560.

TERRY: Let's see . . . that's only a 7 percent raise. I got 10 perent last year.

DALE: Actually, it's 7.4 percent this year. Your new salary is the maximum for the job you are in. Your good work has brought you up to the top of the range. We appreciate your contribution.

TERRY: Dale, can I ever make more money in this company?

DALE: You have moved ahead very fast and you have certainly earned your raises. Your new salary is $33,000 per year—a very good salary for the job you are in.

TERRY: Good compared with what?

DALE: Well, it's a good salary for the duties and responsibilities of that job compared with other jobs in our company and compared to pay rates in other companies.

TERRY: How do you decide on the maximum salary for a job?

DALE: We use job evaluation to classify jobs into pay grades. A committee analyzes each job according to the duties, skills, and responsibilities required. That gives us an impartial method for classifying jobs into grades. Then we study salary surveys to set up pay ranges for the grades. Job evaluations guide us to fair pay relationships among the jobs in our company, and salary surveys tell us about pay outside our company. We merge internal fairness and external competitiveness in our salary program.

TERRY: But, that's all about the job. What about the person in the job—me?

DALE: That's where performance appraisal comes in. Your job performance has been outstanding, so your salary has moved up very quickly. Now you have reached the top rate for your job.

TERRY: Does that mean I will not get any more raises?

DALE: I mentioned that one of our goals is internal fairness. We have salary ranges to ensure that each of our employees is paid fairly for his or her job. We also review those salary ranges every year to make sure we stay in line with competitive pay outside the company. When the surveys show that salaries go up, we raise our salary ranges. When the range moves up, you will have opportunity for further merit increases.

TERRY: Well, at least the maximum is not set in concrete forever.

DALE: That's right. And there is another way you could earn more money—promotion. That's what you should be working on. Take those courses we discussed so you can qualify for more advanced technical work. You have shown that you have the potential.

TERRY: OK Dale, I will take those courses. I'm not going to settle for staying where I am—even if you do raise the salary range next year.

➡ **RATE THIS SUPERVISOR'S PERFORMANCE**

Case Study: REACHING MAXIMUM (continued)

Quiz

Rate the supervisor's performance using a scale from A for excellent to F for poor:

1. Gives a clear explanation　　　　　　　　　　　　　　_____
2. Is precise and accurate　　　　　　　　　　　　　　　_____
3. Invites questions　　　　　　　　　　　　　　　　　_____
4. Understands and responds to employee questions　　　　_____
5. Verifies employee's understanding　　　　　　　　　　_____
6. Gives a positive motivational message　　　　　　　　_____
7. Achieves overall results　　　　　　　　　　　　　　_____

Review Commentary

On items 1 and 2, Dale earned a rating of B, very good. Dale repeated the new salary several times and expressed it as a yearly rate in addition to the monthly rate. Dale might also have given Terry a written form or even a penciled note showing the new pay rate.

Rating Dale on item 3, invites questions, was difficult. The open, friendly manner of the conversation clearly welcomed questions and responses from Terry. Dale did not say anything that specifically invited questions, since Terry actively participated in the conversation. However, if the employee sits silent while the supervisor does all the talking, it is not a conversation, and the supervisor needs to probe understanding. Dale deserved a B on item 3.

Item 4, understands and responds to the employee, was worth an A. On item 5, verify the employee's understanding, Dale might have assumed too much. Dale could have asked some follow-up questions to check Terry's understanding. However, there was no hint of confusion, so Dale rates a B.

The supervisor started with a positive tone, repeated it several times, and ended with a positive reminder of action the employee can take. And, the employee agreed. Therefore, on items 6 and 7, Dale should receive an A. Overall, Dale's performance rated an A- in talking with the employee about some difficult and sensitive matters. Let us further examine some of the issues.

Faced with an employee who has reached the top of the pay range, the supervisor might wonder about the third objective of pay management—rewarding pay. Is the company ignoring the important goal of recognizing individual growth and contribution on the job when it sets pay range maximums? Will we lose one of our best employees? Will the employee make less effort in the future? What would other employees think if they knew about it?

The reason for pay range maximums is to keep pay rates reasonably consistent with the first two objectives of pay management: internal fairness and external competitiveness. No system with multiple objectives can be in perfect balance in all cases—thus the compromise.

Almost everyone accepts the idea that some jobs are worth more than others and that there is a limit to what a particular job can be worth to a company. If the employee knows the pay range for the job, reaching maximum will not come as a surprise. However, circumstances may be less than ideal. A new pay plan, a transferred employee, poor memory, or lack of earlier communication might result in an employee not knowing that his or her pay rate is approaching the maximum.

In a more extreme situation, the employee's current pay rate may be *above* a new maximum. That can occur when a company adopts a new pay plan and some current pay rates are found to be out of line. In such circumstances, the company may freeze the over-maximum pay rates until later adjustments bring the pay ranges to that level. Otherwise, the employee receives no further pay increase in that job. Again, clear communication is necessary. Often, the employee knows the pay rate is high for the job and is not surprised when told so.

Note: When giving information about pay rates in writing or orally, be sure to state a yearly salary amount as the *rate* that will apply while the person is employed by the company. It is not a guarantee that the person will remain employed for that period or that the company will pay any amount after employment terminates. Courts have held that a company made a full-year employment contract when the salary was stated as a yearly amount.

Case Study: MARGINAL PERFORMANCE

Performance appraisal is a formal process for rating an employee's work against the standards for the job. It provides time to praise his or her accomplishments and point out opportunities for further improvement. And it provides a written record to justify pay changes and other actions based on performance. When the employee's performance does not justify a merit increase, the supervisor may feel awkward about confronting the employee with a negative message. However, that is part of the job of being a supervisor.

Leslie, the supervisor, has completed Van's performance appraisal and is now going to talk about pay:

LESLIE: Van, by the time we have our next review of your job performance, I hope you will have corrected your attendance problem, reduced your inventory errors, and greatly improved your customer courtesy. In view of the problems we have discussed, you will continue at the same pay rate for this year.

VAN: You mean I don't get any pay increase? Not even a cost-of-living raise?

LESLIE: That's right, Van. We don't give cost-of-living raises. We give *merit* increases based on job performance. To get an increase, your job performance has to be satisfactory or better. And, you know your work has not been up to standard. Do you understand what I'm saying?

VAN: Yeah. But, why no cost-of-living raise? Prices have been going up, and it is hard to make ends meet. Couldn't you just give me a small cost-of-living raise while I work on improving my performance?

LESLIE: Van, let me repeat. Our company does not tie pay to the consumer price index. We keep our pay ranges competitive with other companies in this area. A pay increase must be based on job performance that is satisfactory or better. That's company policy—a good policy. You have an opportunity here, but it is up to you to improve. You will have no pay increase for now. Your next pay review will be in a year. Do you understand?

VAN: Well, that seems like a hard-nosed attitude for the company to take. I suppose old man Benson told you not to give me a raise. He doesn't like me.

LESLIE: Van, the pay rates in this department are *my* responsibility. I make those decisions within the company's policies and guidelines. We have discussed what *you* will have to do to bring your work up to standard. I am giving you a chance to get yourself back on track because I believe you can do it. Sometimes it takes an incident like this to help a person face up to reality. I hope you will look at it that way and start doing the things we talked about. Remember, I am here to help, so feel free to talk with me any time . . . or you can talk to Robin in the human resources department. Any questions?

VAN: Well, I guess I understand. But, I hoped I would get some kind of raise. A year is a long time to wait.

LESLIE: If you make the effort, you can accomplish the needed results. It is up to you to *earn* a merit increase next year. I hope you do it.

Quiz

You might have serious doubts about Van's prospects. However, it is the supervisor whose performance you are asked to rate here. Grade each item from A to F:

1. Explains clearly   _____
2. Is precise and accurate   _____
3. Discusses openly, and invites questions   _____
4. Verifies employee's understanding   _____
5. Gives a positive motivational message   _____
6. Achieves overall results   _____

Case Study: MARGINAL PERFORMANCE (continued)

Review Commentary

Van presented some emotional challenges to the supervisor. However, Leslie did not rise to the bait and kept the conversation on track and away from personal matters. The charge of influence by "old man Benson" almost got under Leslie's skin, but the response was positive, not defensive or argumentative.

Leslie asked the employee if he understood, but often that is not enough. If the issue is complex, it is better to ask the employee to tell you his or her understanding of the situation. That also has the advantage of planting the information more firmly in the employee's mind because he or she has repeated it. Active participation provides faster and better learning than passive listening.

The employee seemed to be an assertive and outspoken person in any situation—perhaps to a fault—so it was easy to engage Van in a conversation.

A shy, quiet person or a withdrawn person might require open-ended questions to make it a real conversation, not a lecture. A person with a different cultural background might seem shy because of a tradition of lowering the eyes and staying silent in the presence of an authority figure. If the employee does not respond when you talk or looks at the ground, you have to work harder to make sure the communication is effective. If language is an obstacle, let the employee select a fellow worker to serve as interpreter. And put the major information in writing so the employee can review it later or have it translated by others. Do not assume the employee understands or accepts what you have said until you get meaningful response. It is up to you to make it happen.

A difficult employee can try the patience of a saint or the professionalism of a supervisor. In this case, Leslie stayed cool and in control. It seems clear that the employee got the message. The results of this session were about as satisfactory as could be accomplished under the circumstances.

Case Study: RANGE ADJUSTMENT

Supervisors have the task of making it clear to the employee that range adjustments are not merit increases. Such a situation can be confusing to the employee, so the supervisor should make an extra effort to ensure that the employee understands and the written records correctly show the reason for the pay change.

Let us see how supervisor Kami explains a range adjustment to employee Jan:

KAMI: Jan, because of your performance, you do not qulify for a merit increase now. However, starting next month, your salary will be increased by $130 to $2,800 per month. That will bring you into line with the new salary range for your job.

JAN: I don't understand. First you said you were not giving me a raise, but now you just said my salary will go up to $2,800.

KAMI: This is called a "range adjustment" increase. It means that the company raised the salary range for your job this next year, so we are raising your salary to fit in the new range. It has nothing to do with your job performance.

JAN: Well, Kami, I'm happy to get any kind of raise—whatever it is called.

KAMI: Just so I can be sure, please tell me how you understand the situation.

JAN: Well, you are not giving me a merit raise. But you are giving me a range adjustment raise—because the company has new salary ranges. It's like I am being hired again. Is that right?

KAMI: Excellent! And, here is a copy of your change of status form showing your current salary, the new salary, and reason for the change.

JAN: Thanks, Kami. I am sure my work will soon come up to your standards, then we can talk about a merit increase at my next review.

KAMI: I believe you can do it.

Case Study: RANGE ADJUSTMENT (continued)

✦ Quiz

	Poor	OK	Good	Not Sure
1. How well did Kami explain the range adjustment increase?	___	___	___	___
2. How well did Kami keep the conversation on track?	___	___	___	___
3. How well did Kami confirm Jan's understanding of the situation?	___	___	___	___
4. Did Kami agree or disagree with the company policy of paying employees at least the new salary range minimum?	___	___	___	___

5. What would you have said differently?

_____
_____
_____
_____

✦ Review Commentary

In this situation the supervisor's emphasis was on building a clear understanding of the technical reason for the change in salary. Kami covered that quite thoroughly in the conversation with Jan. Note especially how Kami asked Jan to restate the explanation. That technique can be quite effective. However, the supervisor must take care that he or she is not talking down to the employee as if to a child.

Kami reinforced the explanation with the written record, a change of status notice, giving a copy to the employee. This can be an effective method to ensure that the employee gets the correct message. However, you should check with your company's human resources manager or payroll manager to determine if you can give out copies of such company documents.

We don't know whether Kami likes the company policy about paying all employees at least the minimum pay rate for the job. And Jan also doesn't know Kami's views on that matter. This was not the place for Kami to discuss opinions for or against a particular policy. In this communication, Kami performed as a professional and as a member of management by sticking to the subject, verifying that the message got through to the employee, and not getting sidetracked on unrelated attitudes or issues.

Case Study: DEMANDS

The supervisor needs to be alert to any dissatisfaction over pay but without displaying excessive anxiety about pay demands. Don't encourage employees' ideas that the way to get a pay increase is to demand it. They then see company management as exploiting employees—rewarding the complainer and ignoring the quietly competent worker. This leads only to low employee morale and weakened leadership.

The problem of pay demands is illustrated by the following case, in which the employee, Taylor, enters the office of the supervisor, Dana:

DANA: What's on your mind, Taylor?

TAYLOR: Dana, I want to talk with you about my pay. I think I'm worth more than the salary I am getting.

DANA: Most of us feel that way at times. Is there something special that's bothering you?

TAYLOR: Yes! Here is a salary survey from a magazine. It shows I should be paid more than I am getting. And I know two other companies in our industry that are hiring people at higher salaries. Everyone I talk with says I could get more money someplace else. I'm thinking of quitting.

DANA: I can see this *has* been bothering you. I'm glad you came in to talk about it—instead of letting it fester. Let's start with the magazine article. I would like to give a copy of the article to Shannon, our human resources director, and ask for a comparison to the surveys we use.

TAYLOR: Oh? Does the company use salary surveys?

DANA: Oh, yes. We use broadly based surveys in our industry and in this area to help set our salary ranges. Our company hires people frequently, and we want to be competitive with our labor market. If you would like to learn more about how we classify jobs into grades and establish salary ranges, Shannon will be glad to show you the process. But, let's get back to the matter of *your* salary.

TAYLOR: Yeah. That's what I came to talk about.

DANA: In looking over your file, I see that your salary is $4,500 per month. That is just over the midpoint of the salary range for your job. Considering your time in the job and your performance ratings, I would say you are doing OK.

TAYLOR: Maybe it's OK for the company, but I could make more someplace else.

DANA: Possibly. There is always some place that pays more. Our company tries to pay salaries that are about at the median—the middle—among other companies. We are not the highest and not the lowest. We try to reward individual growth and contribution with merit raises based on job performance. Then there is also our retirement program and other benefits—all very competitive.

TAYLOR: Maybe there's more to it than I thought. But I still believe I can get more money. Why shouldn't I leave for higher pay?

DANA: Maybe you should, Taylor, if you are unhappy here. You know it is a big decision. You don't want to create a record as a job-hopper. And you know our company, the people, and the work. I'm sure you'll want to think it over carefully.

TAYLOR: Yeah. I don't want to end up in a dull, routine job . . . or get laid off every time some politician decides to shift a government contract to another company.

DANA: Well, you have to decide whether you are getting a fair shake from us or whether some other company would be better for you. But, whether you stay or leave, I'd like to give you some personal advice.

TAYLOR: Personal advice? Like ''Dear Abby'' or what?

Case Study: DEMANDS (continued)

DANA: Taylor, when you want to talk about salary, it doesn't help to use a complaining approach or a threat to quit.

TAYLOR: Why not?

DANA: Some supervisors feel threatened by such a direct confrontation. Some have been known to tell the employee to clean out his desk and leave immediately. That's why the old advice is to talk about quitting only when you have a job to go to the next day.

TAYLOR: I really wasn't complaining or threatening, but I see what you mean. It might have sounded that way. I'll think about what you said, Dana. You have always been honest with me, and I appreciate that. I would like to take you up on the offer to learn more about the company's salary program.

DANA: Fine. I'll call human resources and ask Shannon to set aside some time to show you how the salary program is designed. She can also talk with you about professional salary surveys.

Quiz

	Yes	No
1. Truthfully now, did you feel like telling Taylor to "take it or leave it?"	☐	☐
2. Was it wise for Dana to offer the personal advice?	☐	☐
3. Should Dana have discussed the magazine survey in detail?	☐	☐
4. Should Dana have ignored the magazine survey?	☐	☐

5. What technique was Dana using in this confrontation? _____

6. Who won? _____

Review Commentary

This case was unusual in that the employee used an openly demanding and threatening approach, and had some ammunition in the form of a magazine article. More timid people and more sophisticated people do not use such crude tactics. However, when you have a nose-to-nose confrontation, you have to deal with it. The natural reaction might be to get into an argument, which could add only heat, not light, to the situation.

Telling an employee to "take or leave it" closes the door on further discussion. It is like turning your back and walking away. The employee feels cut off and is left with two choices. The employee might quit, and the company would lose a valuable if annoying worker. On the other hand, the employee might quiet down but nurse a dissatisfaction with the company and the supervisor until some opportunity for retaliation.

In this case, Dana defused the immediate confrontation. By accepting that Taylor felt underpaid, Dana let Taylor blow off some steam. Dana accepted the magazine article as possibly useful to the company (not something to be debated), that some companies pay higher salaries, and that the employee might leave. There was no resistance for Taylor to fight against, and Dana made no promises. Perhaps Taylor learned that Dana could not be intimidated into giving a pay raise.

Clearly, nobody won or lost. The issue of competitive pay was not settled—it never is. As Dana said, there will always be higher paying companies. (No employee has ever told the boss that other companies pay less for the same job.) Dana cooled the situation by acting in a professional manner, so perhaps the company, the supervisor, and the employee all won.

Case Study: INCENTIVE PAY

Introducing a new sales or incentive pay plan, changing an existing plan or resetting individual goals or quotas requires careful communication with employees. Talking about incentive pay can be more complex and sensitive than talking about regular salaries. The *complexity* comes from the incentive plan itself—the definitions and formulas involved in calculating awards. The *sensitivity* comes from the special motivations associated with incentive pay and the suspicions employees may feel about any change.

Even if top management presents a general explanation of a new plan or a major change, the direct supervisor still has a responsibility to talk with the individual employee and to answer questions. *Compensation is a tool of leadership, with the supervisor providing a key link between the company and the employee.*

The supervisor needs to understand the incentive pay plan in detail before attempting to talk about it. If there is a supervisors' orientation, ask the questions your employees might ask and get answers and examples that you can use when needed.

The regional sales manager, Stacy, is meeting with Lou, one of the top salespeople, to discuss the new sales pay plan, territory, and quota changes:

STACY: Thanks for coming in, Lou. I want to make sure you understand the new sales pay plan and how it will affect you.

LOU: I'm glad we can talk about this. I didn't want to say much in the big meeting with the top brass, but I wonder what they are trying to do to us. What was that consultant saying about "less security pay and more opportunity pay?" I don't buy it! I think they have just dreamed up another way to reduce the cost of selling—and that means cutting my earnings. Am I right?

STACY: Whoa! Slow down, I can see you are a little suspicious about the new plan. Frankly, I don't think it's so bad. It might hurt some of the low producers, but I believe you stand to earn *more*. Have you read the plan and the examples at the back?

LOU: I looked it over but how can I earn more if they are going to cut my base salary? Are you going to give me the same double-talk as the top brass?

STACY: It is true you will have a lower base salary, but you have a chance to earn larger commissions—plus the special bonus. Here is an example I worked out showing how your pay could add up for the coming year.

LOU: Well . . . yeah, you do show higher total earnings for the year, but look at the first two months! I can't afford to take a pay cut like that!

STACY: We don't want you to take a pay cut. During the first three months of the new plan there is a guaranteed draw no less than your average monthly earnings for last year.

LOU: Well, that is something, I guess. But I don't want to get into a negative draw balance and owe my future commissions to the company.

STACY: It is a guaranteed draw against commissions for the first three months only. There is no carry over after three months. You will owe nothing to the company.

LOU: Well, OK. The new plan has one thing I do like, commissions based on gross profit. I always get top price for what I sell. Maybe now I'll get some recognition for that in the paycheck.

STACY: Exactly! And the bonus for opening new accounts could add to your income. You have been good at getting new accounts.

LOU: Opening new accounts takes extra time. The new account bonus might help pay for that time, but I am plenty busy with the accounts I have now.

STACY: We know that. And that is why we are reducing your territory to the area shown on this map.

LOU: Cutting my territory? You almost had me believing this pay deal is OK, but now you tell me you're taking away my life blood. I built that territory; those are my accounts. What are you trying to do to me?

Case Study: INCENTIVE PAY (continued)

STACY: Lou, no one is trying to harm you. Under the new pay plan, you can earn as much or more in the smaller territory because you will have a lower quota. The amount you earn is based on the gross profit of your sales *compared with the quota for your territory.* You will spend less time traveling and more time selling. Read the plan carefully and look again at that example I gave you. It is based on the new territory and new quota.

LOU: Well, even if the plan is OK, how do I know the accounting department will not get it all screwed up?

STACY: I know how you feel about making a change, but as we said in the meeting, the company needs to cover our markets better. We want to provide more incentive for our salespeople. Lou, I am sure you will continue to sell and earn at the highest level. I am also sure you will call me if there is any problem.

Quiz

1. Were Lou's suspicions reasonable? _____ Yes _____ No

2. What motivations might have prompted Lou's reaction? _____
   _____

3. How well did Stacy respond to Lou's concerns? _____

4. Stacy did not answer every question raised by Lou. Why not? _____
   _____

5. Why didn't Lou ask questions in the general meeting? _____
   _____

6. Was Lou completely satisfied by Stacy's explanation? _____
   _____

7. Was it a waste of time for Stacy to meet privately with Lou? _____

8. How well does Lou understand the new plan? _____

9. Should top management have done anything differently? _____

10. Should Stacy have done anything differently? _____

✵ Review Commentary

Lou's anxiety, common to many people when faced with a change, arose as suspicion and sarcasm. Achievers such as Lou want to feel in control of their destiny, want clear rules and goals, and want rewards based on their results. When the company introduces anything new, the prospect of change upsets the person's sense of control—producing anxiety.

Hostile remarks or even a threat to quit are emotional, not rational, responses. They may not be reasonable or justified by the facts; however, they do reflect the *feeling* of anxiety and are a last-ditch attempt to restore the lost sense of control. Even when a new pay plan clearly offers higher earnings opportunity, the temporary loss of self-determination may provoke a negative emotional response.

There is no use in saying that the person should not feel that way. Responding to hostility with hostility, threats, or rejection ("Take it or leave it.") would only intensify the employee's anxiety and possibly provoke termination of a valuable employee. The rational response by an employee would be to study the new plan to quickly regain a sense of control and self-determination. The supervisor can accept emotions when they arise, and they start to clarify the desired control, rules, and rewards that the employee wants.

Case Study: INCENTIVE PAY (continued)

If individual information such as new salary, territory, or quotas is to be given, private discussions should be held with each employee as soon as possible after any general announcement, preferably the same day. In that way, each employee receives complete, official information before informal communications (the grapevine) can create greater anxiety with false or distorted stories. If individual discussions are unnecessary, the wise supervisor will still invite any employee with a question or concern about the new plan to come in for a talk.

Using personal examples, as Stacy did for Lou, is an effective method to show how the new plan will work. Familiar figures and details will help build confidence. Showing pay examples under higher and lower levels of performance would further build assurance. Employees respond far better if management also points out a limitation of the new plan than if they discover it on their own.

Stacy seemed to accept and understand Lou's concerns and did not take a defensive approach, argue, or respond to off-the-track comments or questions. Note that Lou did not return to the questions that were merely venting frustration.

The discussion ended on a friendly note. Stacy restated the reasons for the new plan but did not ask for evidence that Lou understood it. Lou's comments, however, indicated that some of the more complex parts of the plan were clear. Stacy did leave the door open for Lou to return with any question in the future. All in all, the supervisor dealt with the sensitive situation with understanding and professionalism.

Case Study: HIRING

Starting pay is an important part of the hiring process. In some companies, the pay program strictly controls the starting rate, with little or no flexibility for the hiring supervisor. In the following case, however, the hiring supervisor is directly involved in determining the rate. **Note,** it says determining, not "negotiating" the hiring rate. More about that later.

Kim, an applicant for an engineering position, has been interviewed and references have been checked extensively by the human resources manager. Kim has also talked with three senior engineering managers as well as the chief engineer, Tracy, who is again talking with Kim:

TRACY: Well, Kim, now that you have talked with some of our people, I hope you have gained a more complete picture of what we are doing here.

KIM: It was interesting to learn how you are applying laser technology. Your company must be a leader in the field. By the way, does every applicant go through so many interviews here?

TRACY: Just the ones who show real promise. We want to be sure that whoever we hire will fit into our organization and make a contribution to the team. The people you talked with were favorably impressed by your grasp of our work. We believe that your training and experience can contribute here. We would like to have you join us an an Engineer III.

KIM: Well, I think I would like working here. This is an opportunity to get in on some really interesting advanced development and application work in lasers. But what does Engineer III mean in terms of salary?

TRACY: The starting salary for that classification normally is $4,400 per month. However, with your education and experience, we can start you at $4,840, 10 percent above the regular starting rate. It is equal to . . . let's see . . . $58,080 per year.

KIM: Well . . . I don't know. You see, I have one offer higher than that . . . and I expect to hear from another company in a few days. I would really like to work here, but I know I could get a higher salary at another company. Could you make it $5,400 per month to start? That would be in line with the other offer I have.

Case Study: HIRING (continued)

TRACY: We generally start people at or near the minimum salary for the job, but we can start you higher because of your qualifications. We have a formal salary program in our company that helps ensure fairness in the pay relationships among our people. And we keep our salary ranges competitive with regular reviews of broadly based salary surveys. If you join us, you will receive salary reviews at least annually. You can expect your salary to reflect your growth and contribution on the job.

KIM: That sounds good—no hassling about salaries. But I have this higher offer.

TRACY: Well, Kim, that is something you have to decide. You have met several of our people, and you have seen some of our work. I believe we have a first-class team of engineers. We have very little turnover. The new opening is because of expansion connected with our new product. You will find this is a good place to work.

KIM: Yes, I am sure of it. Everything I have seen is very impressive.

TRACY: You will get plenty of exposure to the entire technical operation here, not just your own project. And you will get plenty of hard work—that goes with a growing company.

KIM: It is attractive . . . but I don't know about the salary.

TRACY: Salary is important, but there is always some other place that pays more. We know our salary program is both fair and competitive. So are our benefits. That's part of the reason the people you met are working here. Now, I don't want to pressure you. Think it over, if you wish, and then let us know. Meanwhile, we will continue to interview other applicants who have responded to our recruiting.

KIM: Well . . . I think . . . yes, I'd like to accept your offer.

TRACY: That's great! You can start as soon as you want.

QUIZ AHEAD →

Quiz

	Yes	No
1. Should they have discussed salary earlier?	☐	☐
2. Was Kim bluffing about the higher salary offer?	☐	☐
3. Should Tracy have asked more about the other job offer?	☐	☐
4. Should Tracy have raised the company's offer to Kim?	☐	☐

5. How will this discussion affect Kim's attitude toward the company? _____
_____

6. What effect will this discussion have on Tracy's attitude toward Kim? _____
_____

7. What could Tracy have done differently? _____
_____

Review Commentary

The pay issues are similar both for applicants and current employees. The new employee soon becomes part of the total company pay system. If a supervisor strongly wants to hire an applicant, there is risk of overpaying that person in relation to the company's established employees. More cases of internal inequity arise from this cause than any other. And it is a morale killer when employees see new hires coming in at high pay rates.

A formal pay program provides guidelines for the supervisor. From the application, references and interviews, Tracy knew Kim's former salary and qualifications. Tracy had decided on a reasonable salary for the applicant and stayed with that offer, trying to pay fairly—not "buy cheap."

Case Study: HIRING (continued)

Sometimes a supervisor suggests that a salary offer might not be acceptable by saying, "Is that satisfactory to you?" or "How do you feel about that?"—an invitation to negotiate for more. Tracy said nothing to invite negotiation, but the applicant tried to negotiate anyway. Tracy refused to play the game, explaining instead what the company knew about managing salaries. Consistent with that approach, Tracy did not ask about the other job offer. Whether Kim's higher offer was a bluff doesn't matter. Tracy would have nothing to gain in trying to debate the comparative value of the other offer.

In selling Kim on the job, Tracy stressed:

- fairness of pay relationships
- pay ranges that are competitive
- opportunity for individual salary growth
- low turnover rates
- high-quality engineering teams
- job-content considerations

Tracy might have gone into detail about the benefits program, but this company, like most, had an ordinary benefits program. Even exceptional benefits may not prove especially attractive to an applicant. Notable exceptions are stock options or stock alternatives and uncommon benefits such as free travel for airline employees, which should be explained as part of the company's compensation package. Such benefits can have appeal beyond their cost.

When should you discuss pay with a job applicant? The recruiting advertisement, employment agency, or a search firm may mention the approximate range of starting pay. This general information will automatically screen out most people whose qualifications and prior earnings are sharply out of line with the intended pay. When hiring selectively, it is best to avoid detailed discussion of salary with the applicant until three things happen:

1. You have decided you want to hire the person.

2. You know what salary you intend to pay.

3. The applicant is interested in the job.

Discussing salary too early can sound like a desperate offer to hire. That can make it awkward to reject the applicant if you later decide not to hire the person. If the applicant brings up the question of pay, you can delay it by saying, "We can talk about that later, right now I would like to know more about . . ." Or you might say, "If you are the right person for this job, the salary should not be a problem. Now, tell me about your experience in . . ."

As you go through the selection process, you learn enough about the applicant to make your decisions, and the applicant begins to make an emotional investment in the prospective job. A carefully selected applicant rarely turns down the job offer because of pay. After all, he or she wanted a job. If there is a good match between person and job, there should be little difficulty in completing the hiring.

Most people do not want to negotiate, so don't pressure applicants by asking what salary they expect. You, the employer, will determine the salary.

An applicant for a sales or executive position is more likely than others to try to negotiate salary and other aspects of the job. In most such cases, the firm, fair approach shown here by Tracy will work. If not, make written notes of the applicant's requests (demands?) and tell the person you will call him or her after you have discussed the matter with others in management. This lets time work for you and avoids the impression that you gave in too easily and perhaps could have given more. You can then tell the applicant (remember he or she has applied for and wants the job—perhaps desperately needs the job) what items "we" (the company) can agree to and what items are not acceptable. In almost all cases, that will end the negotiation—one way or the other. Be sure to put the agreement in writing, and get the applicant to sign a copy for the company's personnel files.

By avoiding negotiation or quickly and cleanly resolving it, both supervisor and new employee, including Tracy and Kim, can get on with their work. Neither needs to look back and wonder if one took advantage of the other.

WORDS OF CAUTION

The following terms can be hazardous to the financial health of a company:

Per Year

Stating a salary at the annual rate may create an implied employment contract for a full year. The company could be forced to pay the full year's salary even if the employee is laid off or discharged. Instead, state the pay at the hourly, weekly, or monthly rate. Put in writing the company's right to terminate employment at any time, with pay prorated through date of termination.

Permanent

Saying that a job is permanent may create an implied contract for lifetime employment, which could result in a lawsuit for wrongful discharge if an employee is terminated. Use the term "regular" and make it clear that no one has a right to permanent employment in the company.

Probation

Telling an employee that he or she will be on probation for some period may create an implied contract for continued employment once the designated period has passed. Also, the word "probation" may lead supervisors and employees to think that performance standards and criteria for termination will be different after the "probation period." It is best not to make any such designation, but if you must, use "training period, "introductory period," or "initial period." (Terms and conditions of a union agreement may apply instead of these general guidelines.)

SUMMARY

Don't

Evade responsibility or blame others.
Apologize for company policy.
Mislead regarding the reason for a pay action.
Cut off discussion.
Argue about the correctness of a complaint.
Threaten or invite termination of an employee.
Block appeal to another level of authority.
Promise any future pay action or job.
Let personal problems influence pay decisions.
Manipulate job classifications.
Invite negotiation of pay, whether from employee or applicant.
Mention or joke about race, sex, nationality, disability, marital status, or any other personal characteristic that is not related to pay.

Do

Remain as a member of management.
Use "we" when speaking of management or company.
Investigate carefully; decide fairly.
Preserve integrity in the pay system.
Listen so you understand questions and complaints.
Use the acceptant approach.
Retain the initiative.
Encourage and guide employees toward the future.
Explain the pay program and the employee's status in it.
Document in writing the reason for each pay change.
Clarify a range adjustment increase.
Tell the employee if he or she is well paid for the job duties.

Following the guidelines in this book will enhance your stature as a supervisor and will build your confidence and competence in talking about pay.

CONCLUSION

Supervisors have responsibility for an important and sensitive function—talking to employees about their pay. Recognize that deep emotions are involved for all parties—company, supervisor, and employee. The employee's feelings make the task of talking about pay especially sensitive and the wise supervisor knows that dealing with an emotional topic such as pay calls for three keys:

> **CARING**
> **CLARITY**
> **CONSISTENCY**

▶ The employee knows you care when you

- take time
- talk in private
- listen
- accept feelings
- understand

without necessarily agreeing with the employee.

All of this helps build loyalty and respect for you as the supervisor and member of the company's management.

The employee learns the facts about pay when you:

- plan your talk
- present it clearly
- use plain language
- include examples
- ask questions to test understanding
- provide written documentation

▶ The employee sees consistency and fairness when you:

- explain how the company's pay system works
- operate by facts and policy
- stick to your decision
- avoid special deals for special people

When new facts enter or old policies no longer work, you take the initiative to get the changes that will help your company continue to be a good place to work.

OVER 150 BOOKS AND 35 VIDEOS AVAILABLE IN THE 50-MINUTE SERIES

We hope you enjoyed this book. If so, we have good news for you. This title is part of the best-selling *50-MINUTE*™ *Series* of books. All *Series* books are similar in size and identical in price. Many are supported with training videos.

To order *50-MINUTE* Books and Videos or request a free catalog, contact your local distributor or Crisp Publications, Inc., 1200 Hamilton Court, Menlo Park, CA 94025. Our toll-free number is (800) 442-7477.

50-Minute Series Books and Videos Subject Areas...

Management
Training
Human Resources
Customer Service and Sales Training
Communications
Small Business and Financial Planning
Creativity
Personal Development
Wellness
Adult Literacy and Learning
Career, Retirement and Life Planning

Other titles available from Crisp Publications in these categories

Crisp Computer Series
The Crisp Small Business & Entrepreneurship Series
Quick Read Series
Management
Personal Development
Retirement Planning